SEE

UNDER THE SEA

SEYMOUR SIMON

SCHOLASTIC INC.

New York Toronto London Auckland Sydney
Mexico City New Delhi Hong Kong Buenos Aires

To Joyce ,
with love from all of us,
Seymour, Rob & Nicole, Mike & Debra, Joel & Benjamin, Chloe & Jeremy

ACKNOWLEDGMENTS

Special thanks to Ron Labbe of Studio 3D for his expertise and 3D photo conversions. Thanks also to Alison Kolani for her skillful copyediting. The author is grateful to David Reuther and Ellen Friedman for their editorial and design suggestions, as well as their enthusiasm for this project. Also, many thanks to Gina Shaw and Jenne Abramowitz at Scholastic Inc., for their generous help and support.

PHOTO CREDITS

Front cover and page 9: © Norbert Wu/norbertwu.com; pages 1, 3, 8, 10-11, 20, 21, 22, 23, and 24: © Mark Blum; pages 4-5: © Tom Brakefield/Corbis; pages 6-7, 14-15, 18, and 19: © Robert Bloomberg.; pages 12-13: © Georgette Douwma/Photo Researchers, Inc.; pages 16-17: © British Antarctic Survey/Photo Researchers, Inc.

Book design: Ellen Friedman

ISBN-13: 978-0-439-86656-9
ISBN-10: 0-439-86656-1

12 11 10 9 8 7 6 5 4 3 2 1   8 9 10 11 12 13/0

Printed in the U.S.A.
First printing, March 2008

More than a million kinds of amazing animals and plants live underwater. So it's a good thing that oceans cover about 70 percent of the Earth's surface. In fact, Earth is the only planet in our solar system with liquid water on its surface.

Earth has five named oceans: the Pacific, the Atlantic, the Indian, the Arctic, and the Southern Ocean, which surrounds Antarctica. Although they have different names, all of the oceans flow into one another.

Whales are the largest animals in the ocean—and in the world! The biggest whales are longer and heavier than the largest dinosaur that ever lived. A giant blue whale may weigh as much as twenty-five full-grown elephants. Its heart is as big as a small car.

This killer whale is breaching—leaping straight up out of the water with most of its body and twisting around to crash down on its back or side. Imagine the gigantic splash a whale makes!

FUN FACTS

A humpback whale can grow to be as long as a big bus and heavier than a loaded cement mixer.

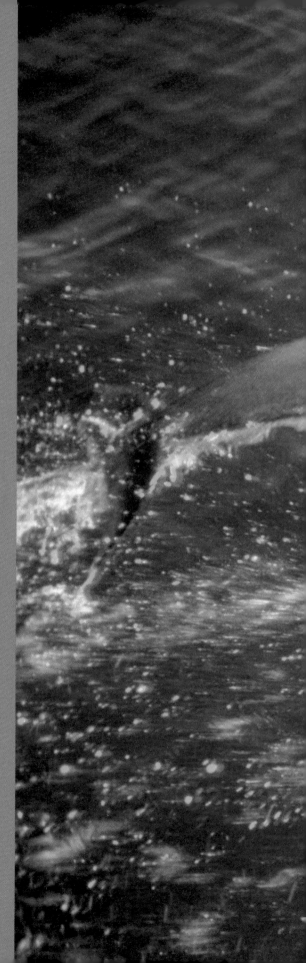

Like whales, dolphins are air-breathing mammals found in all the oceans. They live in groups called pods. Sleek and perfectly shaped to move quickly through the water, dolphins swim at speeds of up to 20 miles per hour and can leap high into the air.

Dolphins are very intelligent animals. Their brains are larger in proportion to their body weight than any other animal, including humans. In captivity, dolphins can learn complicated spoken commands as well as sign language.

A shark's mouth is crowded with sharp, pointed teeth. Some sharks can bite hard enough to make a hole through the steel hull of a small boat.

Sharks often lose their teeth when they bite, but they never run out of teeth. That's because sharks have as many as twenty rows of teeth, with a row of full-grown teeth in front and smaller developing teeth at the back. The new teeth move forward when the old ones are lost or damaged. Sharks can replace thousands of teeth throughout their lives.

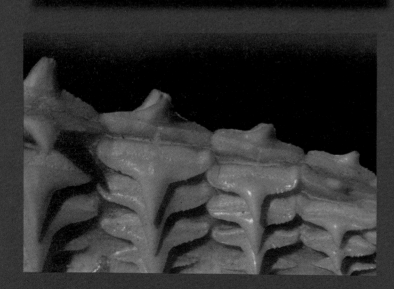

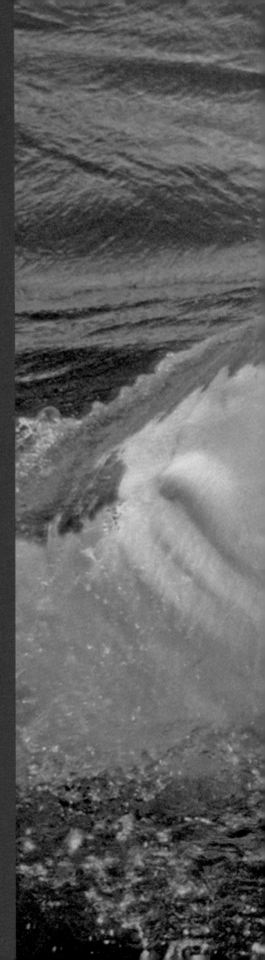

The great barracuda is sometimes called the "tiger of the sea" and lives in warm ocean waters all over the world. Sleek, fast, and powerful, these giant fish can grow to a length of more than 7 feet and weigh more than 100 pounds. Even though this barracuda is very large, it can dash through 40 feet of water in a single second.

While barracudas usually eat fish, the great barracuda has sometimes been known to attack people. Its mouth is huge and filled with razor-sharp teeth.

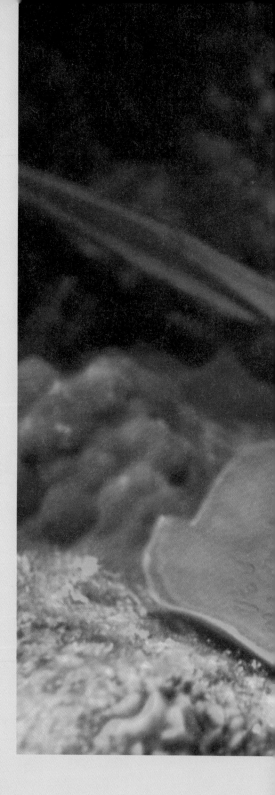

Manta rays are closely related to sharks, but they are harmless to people. They're huge, with a wingspan of nearly 30 feet and weighing as much as 3,000 pounds. Mantas have no teeth—for food, they filter tiny animals from the water as they swim. Two large flaps on either side of its head funnel water through the manta's mouth as it gracefully flaps through ocean water.

Stingrays are much smaller than mantas, but they can be dangerous to people. They often swim in warm, shallow water, and sometimes bury themselves in the sand to camouflage their bodies. Usually, a stingray will swim away if a person comes near. But if you step on it, its poisonous stinger can cause a painful wound.

Moray eels have powerful, muscular bodies that may reach over 10 feet in length. Their strong jaws are armed with long, sharp teeth that are perfect for tearing and holding on to their prey, which can include other fish and octopuses. Morays live in the cracks of rocks, coral reefs, or old shipwrecks in warm ocean waters all over the world. They remain hidden from view until their prey comes close enough for them to strike.

Morays do not hunt people, but they will attack if a person gets too close. A moray bite is painful, but it's not poisonous and is only rarely deadly.

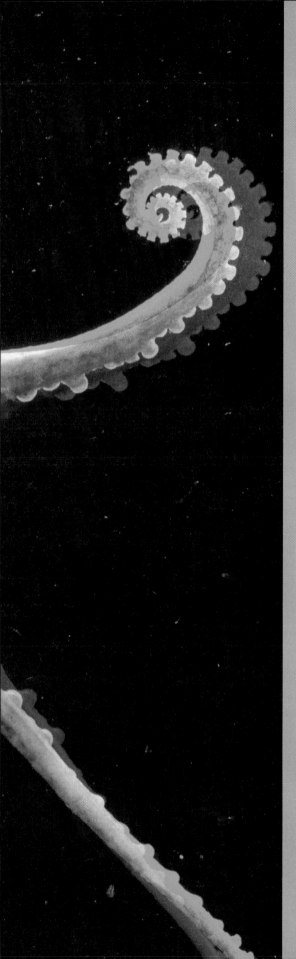

Octopus means "eight feet" in Latin. All of the more than 100 known kinds of octopuses have eight arms covered with suckers. The California octopus is the smallest octopus in the world. It's about the size of your thumbnail and lives in the waters along the Pacific coast of the United States. The giant octopus stretches more than 20 feet from arm tip to arm tip and weighs over 100 pounds. The giant octopus lives in shallow waters from California to Alaska and along the Aleutian Islands across the Pacific to the coast of Japan.

FUN FACTS

Octopuses are usually very shy and will hide or flee if a person comes too close.

Seals and sea lions are mammals that live in the sea. The main difference between them is that sea lions have external ears and seals do not. Most seals and sea lions eat fish and squid and live in cold ocean waters around the world.

Leopard seals are large, fierce hunters that live in Antarctic waters, where they prey on penguins as well as smaller seals. Elephant seals, like the one below, have large noses that resemble an elephant's trunk. Elephant seals are the largest seals in the world. An adult male can grow to over 13 feet in length and weigh up to 4,500 pounds.

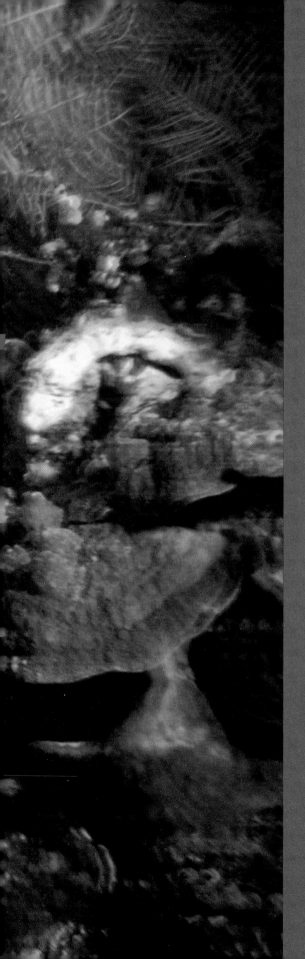

Colonies of millions of individual corals form a coral reef. Each living coral animal forms a hard covering of limestone around its body. Coral reefs grow near the surface of tropical oceans, where sunlight can penetrate the water.

Reefs are home to an astounding variety of tropical or reef fish, such as angelfish, parrot fish, damselfish, and butterfly fish. Shrimp, lobsters, crabs, starfish, sea turtles, and sea snakes also live in coral reefs.

The lionfish is a poisonous reef fish that often floats almost motionless near caves and cracks of a reef, waiting for small fish to come close. This fish has venomous spines that can cause severe pain but rarely lead to death in humans.

Spiny lobsters also live in reefs. They are invertebrates, which means that they have no backbone or inside skeleton. They have a tough outside casing, or exoskeleton, which protects them and supports their bodies. Lobsters shed and replace their exoskeleton with a larger one as they grow.

Oceans are our planet's life-support system, helping to make the atmosphere in which humans, animals, and plants can live. The vast ocean waters that cover so much of Earth's surface help make weather and climate. Millions of people also rely on the oceans for food. Oceans make it possible for life as we know it to exist on Earth.